Reading Worl
Discovery Wo

**LEVEL 1**

GW01397946

# Lots of legs

## Clare M.G. Kemp

Series Editor – Jean Conteh

**MACMILLAN**

## To the Teacher
## or Parent

This simple book is about different animals and birds and the kinds of legs they have. You can use it in many ways to help young children to learn to read. It can also help older children, who can read a little, to become better readers. The book will help young children to learn the names of different birds and animals and to observe them more closely.

You, or an older child, could share the book with a young child, or a small group of children.

- Begin by talking about the pictures on the cover. Ask the children to tell you what they can see, and what they think the book might be about.

- Ask the children what animals and birds they know, and whether they know their names in English. Talk about their names in the children's own language, as these are likely to be more familiar.

- Then, go through the book page by page helping the children to discover that they can guess the whole animal from the part they see first.

- Read all the words aloud.

- You could then ask the children to repeat after you, or to point to individual words as you say them.

- When you have finished reading the book with the children, there are some activities on pages 22–24. These are fun to do and can help them learn.

The words and sentences are very repetitive. This should help the children to identify the words, and perhaps read the sentences independently after practice.

Above all, help the children to enjoy this book. In this way, they will become interested in reading and will want to learn more and become independent readers.

Which animal has big legs?

An elephant has big legs.

Which animal has small legs?

A mouse has small legs.

Which animal has fat legs?

A hippo has fat legs.

Which bird has thin legs?

A flamingo has thin legs.

Which animal has hairy legs?

A monkey has hairy legs.

Which bird has smooth legs?

An ostrich has smooth legs.

# Which animals have four legs?

Cows, goats, cats and dogs have four legs.

Which birds have two legs?

All birds have two legs.

Which animals have no legs?

Fish and snakes have no legs.

How many legs do you have?

1  How many animals can you see?
How many legs can you see?

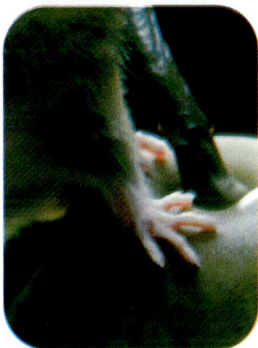

2  Can you find the right legs for the animals?

23

**3** Match the animals to their names.

hippo

ostrich

mouse

snake